AF479997

CHESS FOR KIDS

My first chess book
to learn how to play and win

Pavel Ganchev

Index

Introduction

Hello, little chess geniuses!

In your hands, you have a book full of magic and fun; together, we are going to discover this incredible game; let's start learning and having fun.

Chess is like a huge puzzle with special pieces, with magic pieces that run across the board in a special way; try to capture your opponent's king, and all your pieces will help you.

Not only will we get to know the queen, rooks, bishops, knights, pawns and king, but we will also discover how they can help us win a game of chess.

For this, we will train ourselves in the art of planning moves, protecting our pieces and looking for every possible opportunity to win so we will be the masters of the board!

This interesting game develops our thinking and directs it towards intelligent decision-making, something very important for every aspect of our lives.

Let's start learning to play chess! Let's have fun; it doesn't matter if we win or lose; the important thing is to enjoy each game and learn something new in each one of them.

It's time to get started! Find your board and pieces and get everything ready to discover new and exciting challenges.

Chapter 1

The wonderful world of chess

I welcome you to the magical world you are about to discover!

In this chapter, we are going to learn what chess is, what its history is and what are the benefits of playing it.

We will discover a wonderful game with a simple grid board and some special pieces, which will make us spend many hours of healthy entertainment and great learning.

1.1. What is chess?

Chess is an exciting and fun game, which consists of a square board with black and white squares, where our pieces and those of our opponent move in a special way.

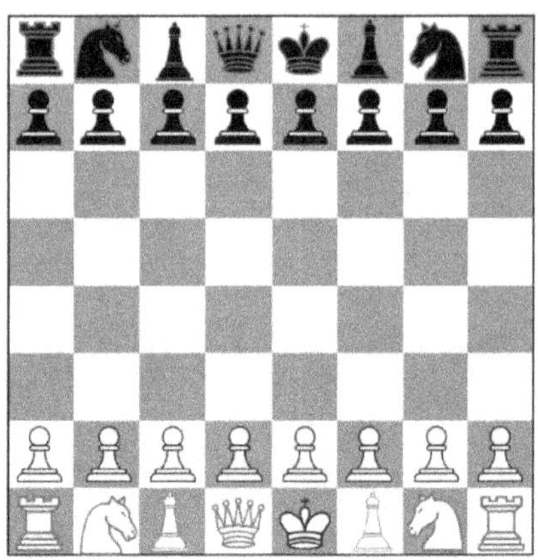

Each of the two players faces each other with the same army and number of pieces, i.e. each player has an army of 16 pieces:

- 1 King.
- 1 Queen.
- 2 Towers.
- 2 Bishops.
- 2 Knights.
- 8 Laborers.

The objective of the game is to protect our king from the attacks of the other player while trying to capture his king; in other words, the winner of the game is the first one who manages to checkmate the opponent's king.

In chess, there are three types of possible outcomes: win, draw and loss. I will tell you a little about them now and, in the course of the book, I will describe them in a little more detail:

1. Victory: Occurs when a player checkmates the opponent's king. When this happens, the player who checkmates wins the game. It is as if he has succeeded in trapping his opponent's king.

2. Tie or "Draw": Occurs when neither player achieves victory or is defeated. There are several types of draws:

   a. Drowned: Occurs when a player has no more moves available and his king is not in check. It is as if he has escaped from being captured, even though he has no available moves.

b. Triple repetition: Occurs when the same position is repeated three times. This means that the players have repeated a series of moves and achieve no changes in the game.

c. Rule of 50 moves: Occurs when there is no piece capture or pawn move for 50 consecutive moves.

d. Mutual agreement: Occurs when both players agree to a draw.

3. Defeat: A player loses when his opponent checkmates his king; this means that his king has been captured and cannot escape.

In chess, victories and defeats are part of the game; each result will give us a valuable opportunity to learn new tactics, improve our game and enjoy each game.

As you may have guessed, this is a game of strategy, which requires planning since in order to anticipate our opponent's moves, it is necessary to think about each of our moves and foresee what the other player's response will be.

There are moves we can make to attack and capture our opponent's pieces, but it is also necessary to make strategic moves to defend our own pieces.

1.2. Brief history of chess

Chess is very old; it has been played by thousands of people all over the world for many years.

It is estimated to be more than a thousand years old; it began in India and then, over time, conquered other countries. During this time, the game has had changes and modifications in its form and rules, but it has always been a lot of fun.

This is why, throughout history, it has become a very popular game, many people play it and great champions have dedicated themselves to chess full-time.

Nowadays, chess is a universal game; it is played all over the world and there are even international competitions and tournaments to find the best chess players.

In the following section, we are going to discover all the benefits we can get from playing chess.

1.3. The benefits of playing chess

Playing chess helps to exercise the memory of young and old, we concentrate better and it helps us to have more patience.

It also develops our ability to solve problems, as it forces us to think of several strategies to face our opponent, defend our pieces and find the formula to win.

This helps us to be creative and to discover alternative solutions in different situations, which in turn strengthens our critical thinking, which will be very useful in many aspects of our lives.

On the other hand, it is a nice way to develop our confidence and self-esteem while socializing by playing with friends and family, participating in tournaments and meeting other players.

Finally, learning to play chess allows us to:

1. Raise our IQ.
2. Improve our mathematical reasoning.
3. Enhancing our memory
4. Develop our capacity for analysis and synthesis.
5. Planning and forecasting to make strategic decisions.
6. Enjoy a fun activity.

In this first chapter, we have learned what chess is, its history and some of its benefits. Now, let's get ready to play.

The fun has just begun!

Chapter 2.

Getting ready to play

In this chapter, we are going to learn the most important information to start playing and prepare ourselves to become true chess experts.

We will learn all about the board, the pieces and their characteristic moves, how to place the pieces on the board at the beginning of each game, and how to form a powerful army to defend our king and attack the opponent.

At the end, we will review some basic moves to understand how to use simple strategies in our games.

2.1. The board and the pieces

Let's start by getting to know the board where we will play chess, the chessboard:

- It can be made of hardwoods such as walnut, oak or maple; there are also plastic boards and magnetic boards, which allow the pieces to adhere and stay in place during the game.
- It has 8 rows and 8 columns that form a unique checkerboard pattern across the board.
- It has 64 squares, alternating between black and white.

All the squares on the board have a specific order. To be able to recognize them, the first thing you must do to identify them is to imagine that you are looking at the board from the front:

- Horizontal rows or lines running from one side to the other.
- The columns or vertical lines running from top to bottom.

Now, so that you can remember the order of the boxes:

1. Start at the bottom of the board. The first column on the left is "a", then "b", "c", and so on until you reach column "h".

2. Then, look at the lowest row on the board, the one that is closest to you, that's row number 1. Then, we go up to row 2, row 3, and so on until we get to row 8, which is the highest row on the board, the one furthest away from you.

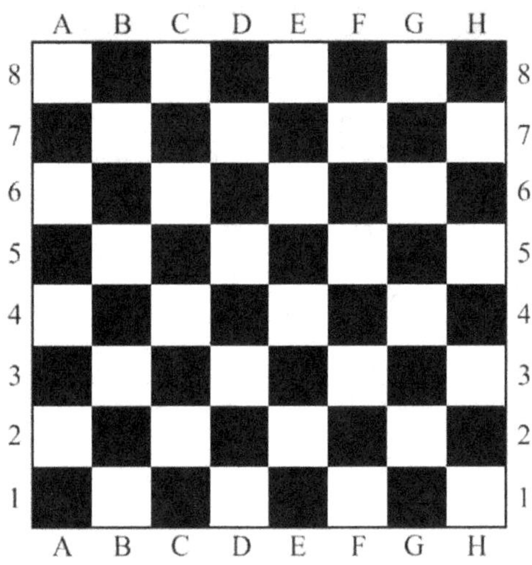

Each box is identified by a name consisting of a letter and a number.

For example, the square in the lower left corner is called "a1" and the square in the upper right corner is called "h8".

Now that we are familiar with the chessboard, let's start discovering the chess pieces.

This set has 32 pieces; 16 are white and 16 are black. Like the board, they can be made with materials such as: wood, plastic, metal or glass.

At the beginning of a game, each player chooses or is assigned the pieces of a color, which he/she will keep until the end of the game; in any case, the white pieces will always start the game.

The decision to choose the color of the pieces that each player will have depends on the type of game:

- In official competitions, a draw is made; a white and a black pawn are placed in a bag, and then each player selects one and plays the pieces of the color of the pawn he/she has drawn from the bag.

- In informal or casual games, players agree among themselves the color of the pieces they will play with.

No matter what color you choose for your pieces, the color does not give any kind of advantage in the game; both colors have the same chance to win the game; it all depends on the skill, ability and strategy of each player.

Not all 16 pieces are the same; there are 6 different types. Each type has a different shape, different way of moving and a specific position at the beginning of the game.

Each chess piece is special; each has an important role in the game, and they are like our brave soldiers.

The 6 types of parts are:

Towers: Each player has 2. They are tall and straight pieces, usually represented by the figure of a medieval fortress. They are placed in the corners of the board.

Knights: Each player has 2 **knights**, usually in the shape of a knight's head, so they are quickly distinguishable. They are placed next to the towers.

Bishops: Each player has 2; they are thin diagonal pieces with a notch at the top, usually resembling a pointed hat or a miter. They are placed next to the knights.

Queen: Each player has 1 queen, his most powerful piece; it is taller and more elegant than the other pieces; it resembles a crown. It is placed on the central square of its color, i.e. the white queen goes on the central white square, while the black queen goes on the central black square.

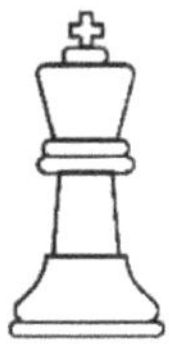

King: Each player has 1 king. The king is the most important piece and the object of the game is to protect it; usually, its design has a solid and wide base; at the top, it is shaped like a crown or pointed hat, then it narrows and ends with a small cross at the top. The king is placed next to the queen.

Pawns: Each player has 8 pawns. They are the smallest pieces and usually have a small, rounded head on top. They resemble soldiers since they are the first line of defense of our army, but they can also become more powerful pieces. If each player sees the board, they will be placed in the second row closest to him, just in front of his other pieces.

Both the board and the pieces help us to visualize our moves and plan them. They are our battlefield and army.

In the next section, we will learn how to place the pieces on the board at the beginning of the game.

2.2. How to place the pieces on the board

When starting a game, each player must place his pieces on the board, so it is very important to know where each one should go; so now, we are going to learn how to place them and get them ready for the battle.

In the first two rows closest to us, we will place our army of pieces, while our opponent will place his in the two rows farthest from us.

The order to place our pieces starts in the row closest to us, as follows:

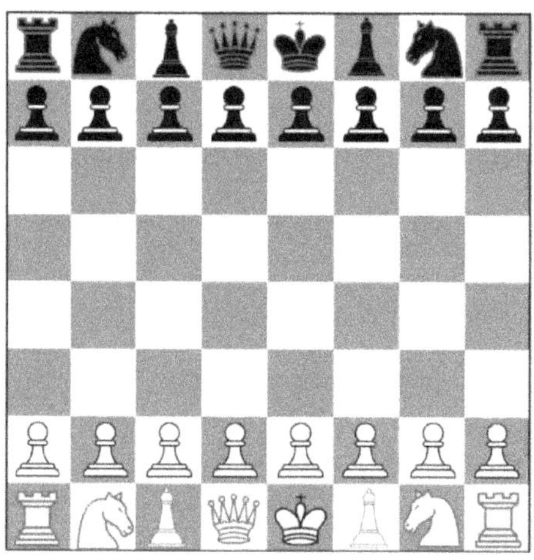

The towers are at the corners:

- White on squares a1 and h1
- Black on the squares a8 and h8.

At his side are the Knights:

- White on squares b1 and g1.

- Black on squares b8 and g8.

Next come the bishops:

- White on squares c1 and f1.
- Black on squares c8 and f8.

The queen goes on the central square of its color:

- White on the white square, square d1.
- Black on the black square, square d8.

We complete this row by placing the king next to his queen:

- White on the e1 square.
- Black on the e8 square.

Next, we continue with the second row, which is where we will place all our pawns, just in front of the pieces we have already placed, like this:

- White between the squares a2 and h2.
- Black between the squares a7 and h7.

Once we have placed all our pieces, and our opponent has placed all his, the board will be ready to start a new and interesting game.

In the following section, we will learn about the nomenclature used to identify squares, pieces and moves, something very useful to facilitate communication between players.

2.3. Chess Nomenclature

Chess uses a nomenclature formed with letters and numbers to describe the squares, the moves of the pieces and their position.

This nomenclature has several rules so that its use is uniform and so that all players can communicate with each other.

Nomenclature of the board squares

As we have seen previously, the chessboard has 64 squares, each of them identified with a lowercase letter and a number, which allows us to locate the pieces and the moves on the board.

The letters go from "a" to "h" and represent the columns, while the numbers go from 1 to 8 and represent the rows.

For example, the square in the lower-left corner of the board is called "a1", and the square in the upper right corner is called "h8".

Nomenclature of parts

Each piece in chess, with the exception of pawns, has an associated letter that is uppercase for white pieces and lowercase for black pieces. These letters are:

- King: K (white), k (black).

- Queen: Q (white), q (black).
- Tower: R (white), r (black).
- Knight: N (white), n (black).
- Bishop: B (white), b (black).
- Pawn: It is not represented by any letter; it simply indicates the square to which it moves.

For example, with the following notation, you can identify that the white rook is located on the square "a1", it is very simple:

- Indicates the piece: The white tower is represented by the letter "R" (capital letter).
- Indicate the square where it is located: The white rook is on square "a1".
- Gather all the information: "Ra1".

If you want to identify that the black rook is on square "a1", it is also very simple:

- Indicates the piece: The black rook is represented by the letter "r" (lower case).
- Indicate the square where it is located: The black rook is on square "a1".
- Gather all the information: "ra1".

Nomenclature of the moves

There are several types of nomenclature used in chess to describe the moves during a match; the most popular are descriptive and algebraic notation, both of which describe the moves by combining the letter of the piece and the target square.

Descriptive notation includes the use of words to describe the movement of the pieces, using the name of the piece, the name of the initial column, the word "a" and the name of the final square to describe the movement of the piece.

For example, if the white queen moves from column e to the square located in column f and row 8, it is written "White queen from e to f8".

In this case we can see that:
- The name of the piece is: White Queen.
- The initial column is: e.
- Includes the word "a".
- The final square is: f8.

On the other hand, algebraic notation describes the movements of the pieces using the letters that represent each type of piece, together with the letter and number of the square to which it moves.

For example, with the following notation, you can describe the movement of the white rook from the square "a1" to the square "a8":

- Indicates the square of origin: As the white rook is on square "a1", "Ra1" is written.
- Indicates the destination square: As the white rook moves to the square "a8", it is written "a8".
- Gathering all the information, the white rook's move from square "a1" to "a8" can be described as "Ra1-a8" (a dash or an arrow should be used to separate the square of origin from the square of destination).

If the piece is black, remember to use the letter that identifies it in lower case, following the previous example, to describe the movement of the black rook from the square "a1" to the square "a8" we would write: "ra1-a8".

Chess nomenclature is a standardized form of communication between players, helping them to identify pieces, squares and moves clearly and precisely.

In the next section, we will learn the basic movement of the pieces and we will be almost ready to dominate the board!

2.4. Basic movement of parts

Each type of piece moves in a different way; let's see how each one moves on the board.

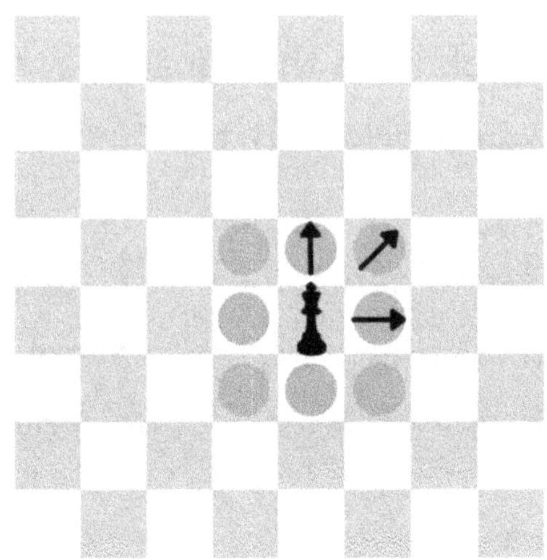

2.4.1. The King

It can move in any direction: forward, backward, sideways and diagonally, only one square at a time, as long as it is not in danger of being captured by the opponent.

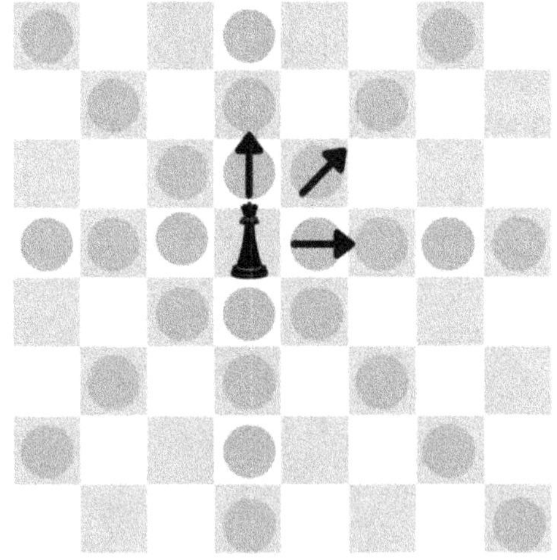

2.4.2. The Queen

It can move any number of squares in any direction: forward, backward, sideways and diagonally. It is the most powerful and versatile piece because of its attacking power, defense capability, board control and participation in strategic tactics.

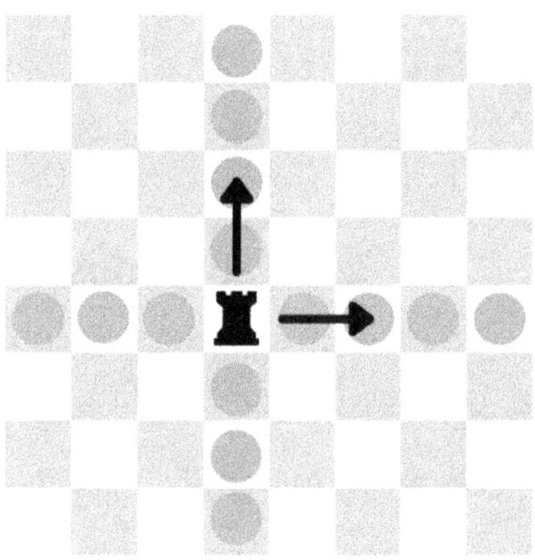

2.4.3. Towers

They can move any number of squares in a straight line: forward, backward and sideways.

They are strong and important, as they can control the columns and rows of the board.

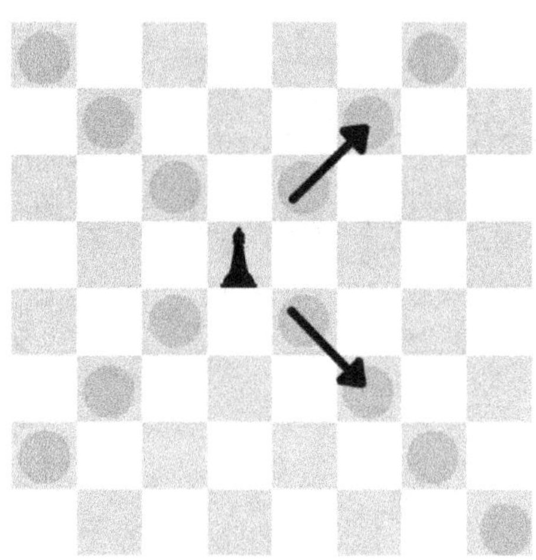

2.4.4. Bishops

They are unique pieces in chess; each one can move any number of squares, but only the color that corresponds to it; this is assigned when placing the pieces on the board before starting the game, ie:

- One bishop is located on the white square and
- The other is located in the black box.

Both move diagonally, one on the diagonals formed by the white squares and the other on the diagonals formed by the black squares.

They are strategic pieces and help us to control the diagonals of the board.

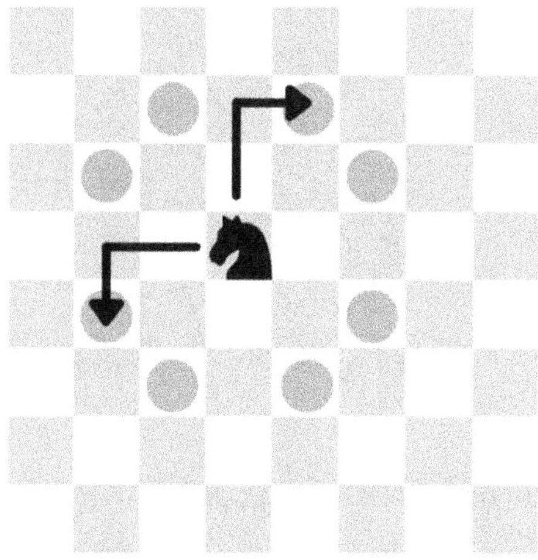

2.4.5. Knights

They are the only pieces that can jump over other pieces, and they move in an "L" shape, advancing two squares in a straight direction and then one square in a perpendicular direction.

2.4.6. Pawns

Pawns always move forward, they do not move backward, but they have some peculiarities:

- When moving each pawn for the first time, they can advance one or two squares, depending on our game strategy.
- After their first move, they may only advance one square at a time.

- They can only capture their opponent's pieces diagonally by advancing only one square diagonally.

- The best thing about pawns is that at the other end of the board, they have a chance to promote: they can be exchanged for more powerful pieces captured by our opponent.

Let's take a look at the rules of the game!

2.5. The rules of the game

The basic rules of chess are:

- The player who has the white pieces starts the game. Then, the players alternate to move their pieces.

- If a pawn reaches the last row of the opponent's board, it can be promoted to any other piece that has been captured previously; this piece will be placed in the last position of the pawn that promoted it.

- A player's pieces cannot move to the squares occupied by his other pieces.

- If a piece is moved to a square occupied by the opponent, this opponent piece is captured and removed from the board.

- If the king is in a position where, on the next move, it can be captured, it is in check.

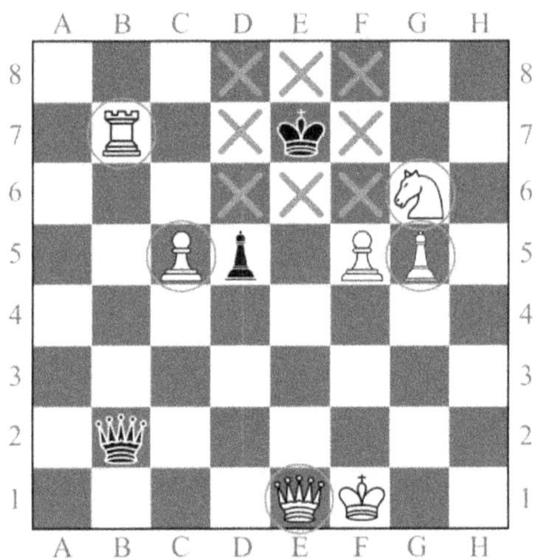

- If the king is in a position where it has no way to escape check, it is in checkmate, loses the game and the game ends.
- The player who captures the opponent's king wins the game.
- As I mentioned before, the game may end in a draw.
- In chess, it is very important to follow the rules and respect the opponent. Players must play fair without cheating, distracting or disturbing the opponent.

In addition to these basic rules, there are advanced strategies and tactics that you will learn as you play.

Continue reading in the next section, where you will learn basic moves that will help you understand this game a little more.

2.6. Examples of basic moves

It is time to learn some basic chess moves. Let's see how to create strategies with our pieces to capture our opponent's pieces.

2.6.1. Control columns and rows

The towers help us to control the columns and rows of the board; some ways to do this are:

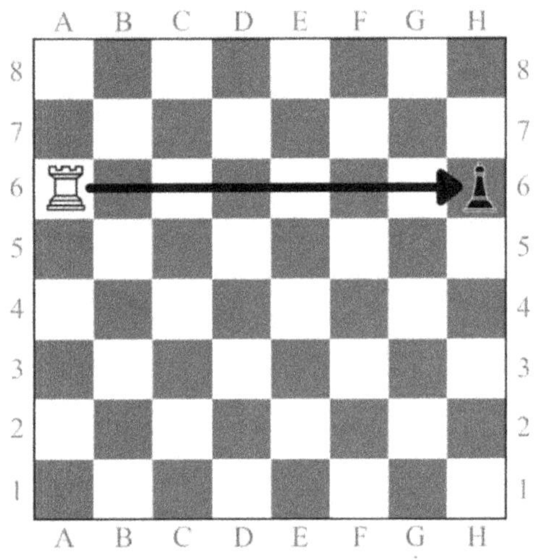

Horizontal movement: In a row, the rook moves to the left or to the right and can attack any piece that is in that path. For example, we can move the rook from column a to column h and capture any opposing piece that is in that row.

Vertical movement: In a column, the rook moves up or down and can attack any piece that is in that path. For example, we can move the rook from row 4 to row 8 and capture any opposing piece that is in that column.

Control of rows and columns: If there are towers in different rows or columns, several lines can be controlled simultaneously and if there are no pieces blocking our way, it will allow us to attack and capture the opponent's pieces.

2.6.2. Controlling diagonals

Bishops help us to control the diagonals of the board.

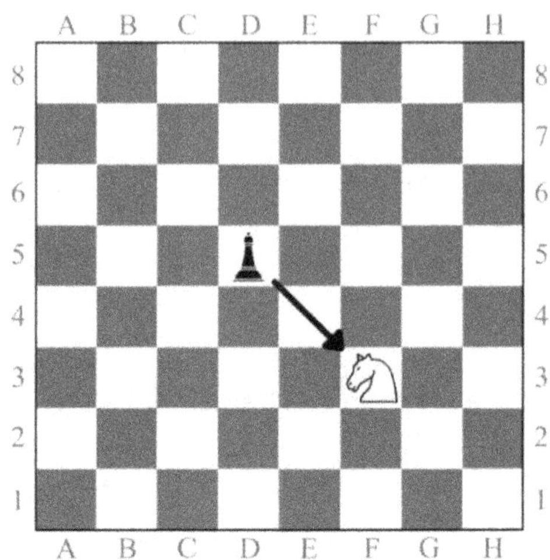

Diagonal movement: A bishop moves in a straight line across the diagonals of the board. For example, if we have a bishop on the d5 square, we can move it to the f3 square and if we have no pieces of our own blocking the way, we can attack and capture an opposing piece.

Control of diagonals: If we have our bishops located in different diagonals, we can control several lines of the board at the same time and if there are no pieces blocking our way, we can attack and capture the opponent's pieces.

Attack at a distance: Bishops can attack pieces at a distance and capture an enemy piece, even if it is several squares away on the same diagonal.

2.6.3. Jumping to attack and capture pieces

Only knights have the ability to jump over other pieces; let's see how we can use them to effectively attack our opponent and capture his pieces.

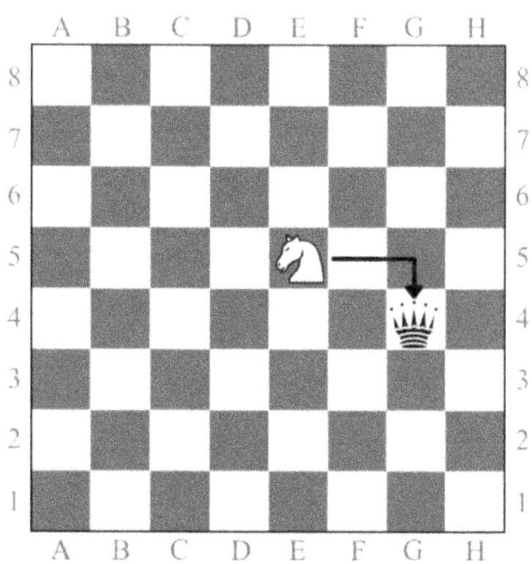

L-shaped move: The knights move in an "L" shape on the board. For example, from the e5

square, we can move the knight to the g4 square.

Jumping over other pieces: Knights with their "L" jump can move even if there are pieces, ours or our opponent's, blocking the way.

Surprise attacks: Knights can jump and surprise the enemy by reaching places that other pieces cannot, so we can take advantage of this to attack and capture pieces by surprise.

2.6.4. Controlling the center of the board

Controlling the center of the board is key in our plan or strategy to win a game. Let's see some examples of how we can use the control of the center of the board to open paths for our pieces, attack and capture our opponent's pieces, and promote a pawn to another piece.

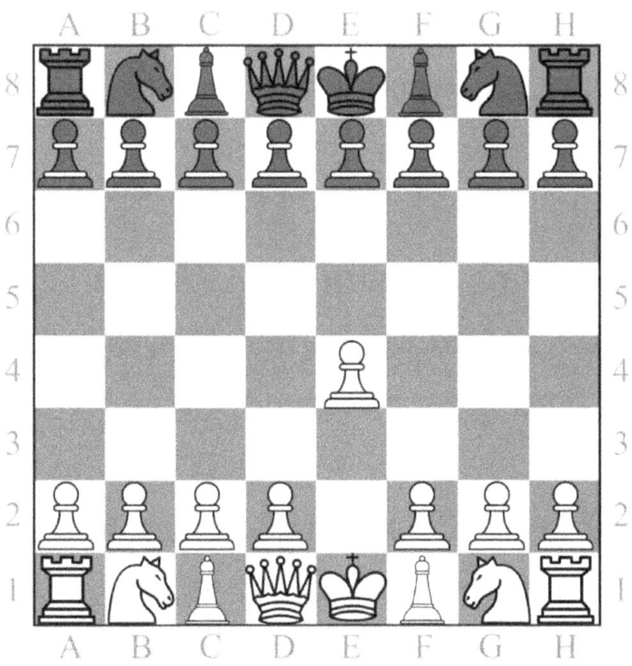

Occupy the center: Moving our pieces to the center of the board gives us more options to create winning moves. For example, we can move our pawn from e2 to e4, so we start to control the center and open the way for our other pieces.

Attack from the center: By placing our pieces in the center of the board, we can attack the other player's pieces in different directions.

For example, if our rook is located on the square d4, we can attack the opposing pieces that are located in columns "d" or on row 4.

Pawn promotion: If we manage to advance one of our pawns to the last row of the board on the opposite side, we can promote it.

With this, we can convert it into a piece that has been captured by our opponent; this could be our queen, rook, bishop or knight; therefore, we will recover a more powerful piece.

2.6.5. Protecting the king and avoiding danger

One of the most important actions we can do when playing chess is to protect our king. Let's see some simple examples of how we can protect our king and avoid dangerous situations.

Castling: In this move, the king and one of the rooks move together to place our king in a safer position, which will be more protected behind a pawn fortress. In chapter 3, I will explain this move in more detail.

Using pieces to defend: We can use our rooks, bishops or knights to defend the king; placing these pieces around him will create a protective barrier.

Observe the opponent's moves: It is very important to be attentive to our opponent's moves, so we can foresee and anticipate any attack he may try against our pieces or any threat our king may suffer.

To keep our king safe, we must avoid placing him in dangerous situations.

Remember that the main objective of the game is to protect the king and avoid his capture. Pay attention to the safety of your king and plan your moves accordingly.

In this chapter, we learned the fundamental aspects of chess. We got to know the board and the pieces, understanding their arrangement and their importance in the game.

We also learned the basic movement of each piece and also saw how to use our pieces in some strategic situations.

Now, we are ready to read Chapter 3, where we will learn how to plan our moves, develop tactics and use strategies to win games.

Chapter 3.

Strategies and tactics

In this new chapter, we are going to learn tricks and special moves which can help us to win more chess games.

We will learn about several tactics and strategies that can improve our game, such as having pieces in the middle of the board, promoting pawns or castling.

We will also learn to think carefully and protect our pieces while trying to capture our opponent's pieces.

Finally, let's review some examples of cunning moves that will give us a great advantage in the game.

Let's start with the next section to find out how to control the center of the board.

3.1. Control of the center of the board

In this section, we will discover how we can control the center of the board and thus, have a little more advantage in the game.

The center of the chessboard is like its heart, and the fact of controlling these squares will give us more strategic game options since it allows us to move them easily to different parts of the board.

With this, we can attack our opponent from different directions and thus, have many more opportunities to capture his pieces.

The squares d4, d5, e4 and e5 are the heart of the board; try to occupy them with your pawns or other pieces to have more space and mobility.

To achieve control of the center of the board, we must take advantage of our moves to place our pawns and pieces towards those squares. By doing this, we will create a barrier that will hinder our opponent's advance towards our territory.

Keep your eyes on the center of the board and look for opportunities to control it and use it to your advantage.

Now that you have learned about controlling the center of the board, let's read with the next section: "Piece development", where we will discover how to promote a piece.

3.2. Promotion of parts

Did you know that pawns can turn into another piece? Yes, this happens when they reach the last row of the opponent's board. It's as if they have superpowers!

When one of our pawns manages to reach the last row of the opponent's board, it can be exchanged for any piece that our opponent has captured.

This is a golden opportunity to improve our army of pieces and increase our chances of winning the game.

Take a look at what would happen if we advance our pawn to the last square on the opponent's end, in this case to the b8 square:

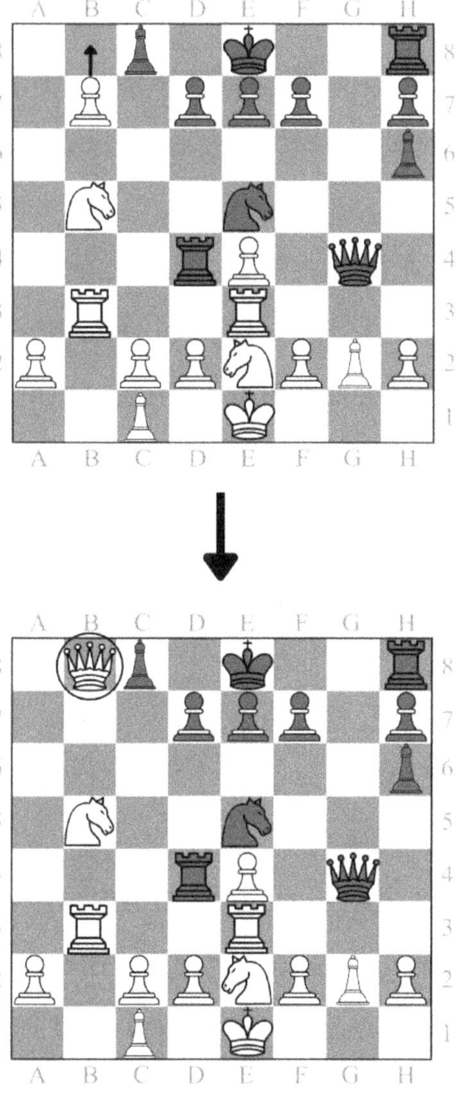

Imagine that one of our pawns has not been captured by our opponent and has reached the last row of the board. At that moment, we can turn it into one of the pieces that our opponent has captured, the one we need the most.

It is important to analyze well which of them we are going to choose, although most of the time, the wisest choice is to promote our queen, a very powerful piece since we can move it several squares in any direction.

However, if our queen is still in the game without being captured by our opponent or in other situations.

It would also be useful to promote a rook, bishop or knight, depending on the board position of the pawn to be promoted and our game plans.

The promotion of a pawn can completely turn the course of the game and provide new opportunities for attacking and defending pieces.

In the following section "Castling" you will discover a special move that will help you to protect your king and ensure that it is safe during the game.

3.3. Castling

Castling is a very important move, since it protects our king and we can ensure that he will be safe during the game. We can say that we are building a fort for him.

Castling consists of moving our king and one of our rooks at the same time, it is a simple move, but it can only be done if certain specific conditions are met.

Castling can only be performed if:

1. Previously, in the game, the king has not been moved.
2. Likewise, the rook involved in the castling must also not have been moved earlier in the game.
3. There are neither our own nor the other player's pieces between the king and the rook.
4. The king is not in check.
5. To castle, the king does not pass through squares that are under attack by our opponent.

There are two types of castling: the short castling and the long castling.

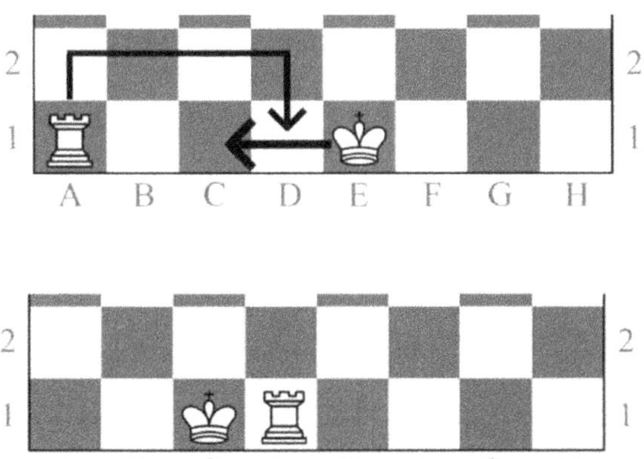

Short castling: The king moves two squares to the nearest rook and this rook is placed on the opposite side of the king. This move is performed on the squares g1 and f1 for the white pieces or g8 and f8 for the black pieces.

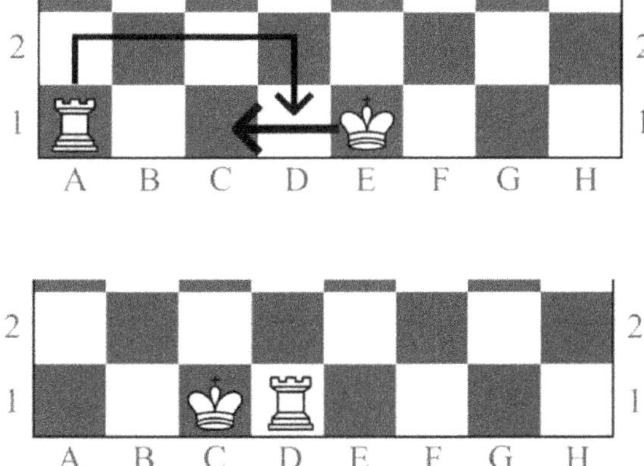

Long castling: The king moves two squares to the farthest rook and this rook is placed on the opposite side of the king. This move is made on the squares c1 and d1 for the white pieces or c8 and d8 for the black pieces.

Castling is a very useful move, since it allows us to put our king in a safer position because it will be away from the center of the board, where it will be more vulnerable to the opponent's attacks; it also allows us to develop the rook and have a better defense.

Continue reading the next section, where we will discover how to plan our moves to attack the opponent's pieces and, at the same time, protect our own pieces.

3.4. Attack and defense

In this section, we will discover the world of attack and defense in chess. We will learn how to plan our moves to attack the opponent's pieces and, at the same time, protect our own pieces.

When we play chess, we must look for opportunities to attack the opponent's pieces and capture them. But we must also be careful and protect our own pieces from the obstacle's attacks.

An important tactic in chess is to create threats to the opponent's pieces. We can threaten an opponent's piece by moving one of our pieces to attack or capture the enemy piece.

This will force the opponent to take defensive measures to protect his threatened piece.

When we attack, we must also be attentive to the possible counterattacks of the opponent. Defense plays a crucial role in chess.

We can protect our pieces by placing them in safe positions or by moving other pieces to block enemy attacks.

A good strategy combines attack and defense in a balanced way. Don't forget to protect your own pieces while looking for opportunities to attack your opponent's pieces.

Continue reading the following section to learn about some tactics that will help us improve our game, such as the dive, the fork and the double threat.

3.5. Examples of chess tactics

In this section, we will learn about different chess tactics that will allow us to have an advantage in the game we play.

By learning and using them, we can surprise our opponent and have a chance to win.

In this section, we will learn three important tactics: the dive, the hairpin and the double threat.

With the pinning, we force an enemy piece to occupy a position from which it will not be able to move, since otherwise, it will expose a much more important and valuable piece for him.

The fork is another powerful tactic; with it, we simultaneously attack two of our opponent's pieces with only one of our own. This will also put him in a difficult situation, since he must decide which of the pieces to save and which to sacrifice.

With the double threat, we simultaneously threaten two of our opponent's pieces with two of our own; this forces him to choose which piece to protect and which to lose.

These three tactics can be used at different moments of the game; all of them give us the opportunity to put the opponent in a difficult situation, take the initiative and have a better chance of winning the game.

Let us now look at each of them in a little more detail, starting with the dive.

3.5.1. Pin

Let's start with an example, if the other player is protecting his king with one of his rooks, it is said that the rook is pinned. In this case, we can move our rook to attack; with this, we force him to decide in a difficult situation, since he should not move because he will leave his king unprotected and vulnerable.

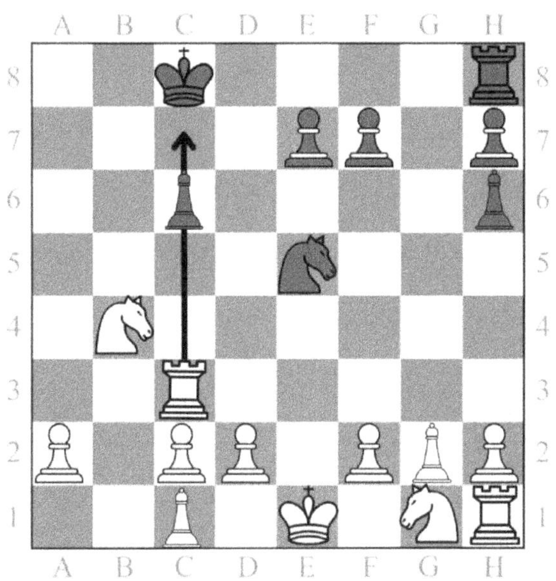

This is why it is important to identify the pieces you use to protect your important pieces; with this information, we can plan our moves and create a situation in which you have to make difficult decisions, for example, sacrificing pieces, and this will give us a strategic advantage in the game.

Pinning can be done with different pieces, but the rook is especially good at this tactic, thanks to its ability to move in straight lines and to attack from a distance.

Watching for pinning opportunities can change the course of the game in our favor.

3.5.2. Fork

In this section, we will discover how we can attack, at the same time, two of our opponent's pieces with only one of our own.

The fork is a powerful move that allows us to put the opponent in a difficult situation since he will only be able to save one of his two threatened pieces and lose the other.

Imagine the following board: you have a knight on the c3 square and another on the e4 square, while the other player has a rook on the b6 square and a bishop on the c5 square.

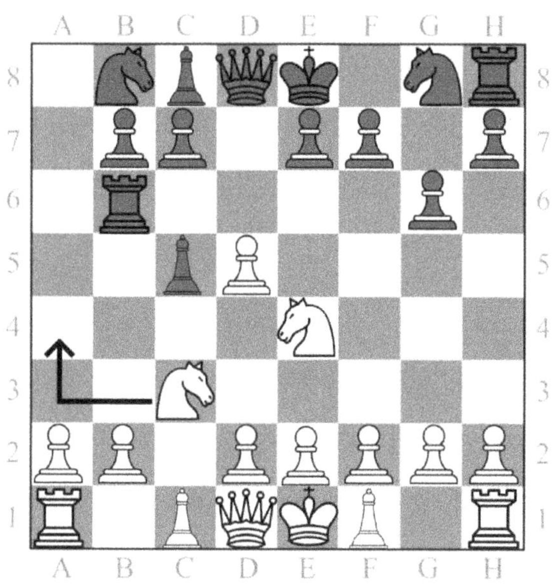

If you move your knight from the square c3 to the square a4, you are making a fork; this means that, with only one of your pieces, you are attacking both the bishop on c5 and the rook on b6. This puts your opponent at a crossroads, since he can only save one of his pieces.

He will have to decide which piece to protect. If he chooses to save his bishop, he will lose his rook, and if he chooses to save his rook, he will lose his bishop. Whatever his decision, you will gain an advantage by capturing one of his pieces.

The key to forking is to take advantage of weaknesses in our opponent's piece placement. It is important to watch for fork opportunities during the game and not miss the chance to gain an advantage.

Another important aspect to consider is that before making the fork, you should think about your opponent's possible moves, how his choice will affect the game and how you can make the most of the situation.

Although it can be done with other pieces, the knight is especially good at this tactic because of its ability to jump.

3.5.3. The double attack

In this section, we will discover how we can threaten two of our opponent's pieces at the same time, putting him in a very difficult situation, since we force him to choose which piece to protect, leaving the other vulnerable to our capture.

You attack with two of your pieces, each one separately threatening one of the other player's pieces, so he can only save one of his pieces; the other remains vulnerable and in danger of being attacked.

Imagine this board: you have a knight on the g1 square and a rook on f3, while your opponent has a bishop on the f6 square and a rook on g5.

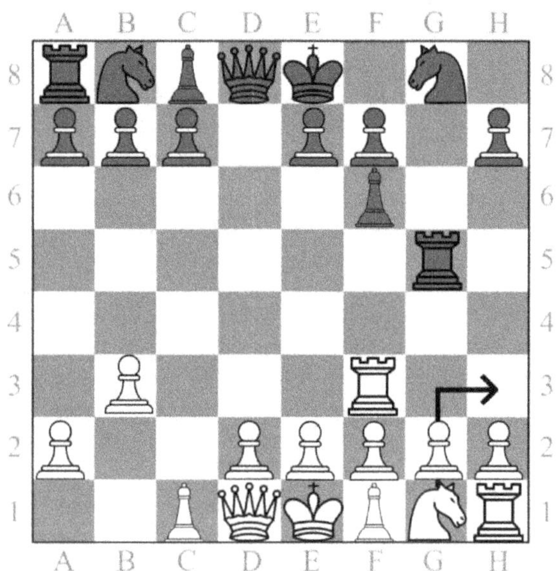

If you decide to move your knight from the g1 square to h3, you will be making a double threat to your opponent, since you are threatening both his bishop on f6 and his rook on g5.

He will have to make a difficult decision. If he protects his bishop by moving it to g7 or e5, he will lose the rook on g5. But if he protects the rook by moving it to h5, he will lose the bishop on f6. Whatever his decision, you will have the advantage of capturing one of his pieces.

Always look for the opportunity to use the double threat tactic during your games and use it to your advantage.

Now, review the tactics we have learned in this chapter. From controlling the center of the board to the pinning, the fork and the double threat, you have already acquired valuable tactical skills for playing chess.

Continue reading the next chapter, where you will learn about the different openings you can use at the start of a game.

Chapter 4.

Openings

In this chapter, we are going to know the most important aspects of the openings; these are the first strategic moves that are made at the beginning of a chess game.

They are like magic keys that, if we know how to use them to our advantage, will open the doors to a successful departure.

We will also learn about some types of openings and how to use them effectively to gain an advantage from the beginning by taking control of the board and preparing to develop our pieces.

We will discover the specific openings, such as the Italian and the Sicilian defense, their secrets and key moves, so that we can wisely plan our moves and surprise our opponents.

So, get ready to discover the secrets of chess openings, start reading the following lesson and get ready to play chess like an expert.

4.1. Concept of opening

In chess, the opening is the initial phase of the game, the moment when we make our first strategic moves in order to establish our position on the board.

Imagine you are playing a game of chess and you are facing your opponent; in the opening, you will be taking the first step to build the fortress that will protect your king from your opponent's attacks during the game.

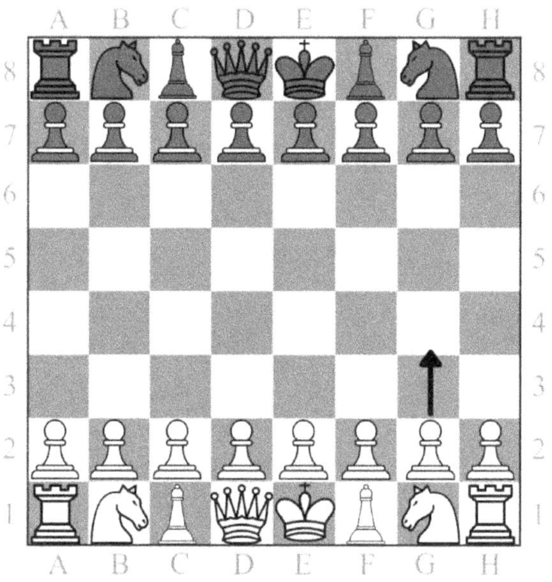

It can be said that it constitutes the basis on which you will build your tactics and strategies throughout the game.

During the opening, it is very important to keep in mind some objectives that are key to have a good start of the game. The first one I am going to tell you about is: Controlling the center of the board.

As we mentioned before, the center is a strategic place on the board, since its domination allows us to move our pieces freely, as well as to have more attack and defense options.

If we manage to occupy the center of the board with our pieces, we will create a solid base with which we can develop our pieces more easily, efficiently and effectively.

Another important objective of the opening is to ensure the safety of our king. As you know, the king is the most valuable piece of our entire army, so we must guard him safely so that he is well protected.

For this, we can make several initial moves that build a defensive shield and allow us to castle our king in a less exposed and much safer position.

On the other hand, in the opening, we must also look for the development of our pieces, or what is the same, to take them from their initial squares to other more active positions on the board.

Remember what we have learned previously, each piece has unique moves that allow them to play a specific role within the game, so we must ensure that each one is ready in a timely manner to play its role during the battle.

The opening is only the beginning of the game, but its role in the game is very important, since it allows us to have a good position from the beginning.

Do not forget that we must also be prepared to adapt our game to the tactics used by the other players and adjust our strategy appropriately as the game evolves.

Now that you know the opening concept, you are ready to start learning the specific openings; let's start in the next section with the Italian opening.

4.2. Italian opening

In this section, we are going to discover a very special opening, the so-called Italian opening; this type of opening is known for its aggressive approach and for its search for a strong position to attack the other player.

This strategy gets its name from Italy, a beautiful country in Europe. Like Italy, this opening has its own beauty and charm in the chess world, but let's talk a little about its technique and what it consists of.

The following nomenclature: "1.e4 e5 2.Nf3 Nc6 3.Bc4" represents the sequence of moves used in the Italian opening.

This nomenclature describes the first moves of a chess game, where the white pieces perform the king's pawn opening, and the black pieces respond with the king's pawn defense and the Italian defense; I will explain in more detail what all this means and what it consists of.

Let's start with the term "1.e4": This term means that the player who opens the game, i.e. the player who plays with the white pieces, moves two spaces forward the pawn located on the e2 square, i.e. advances to the e4 square.

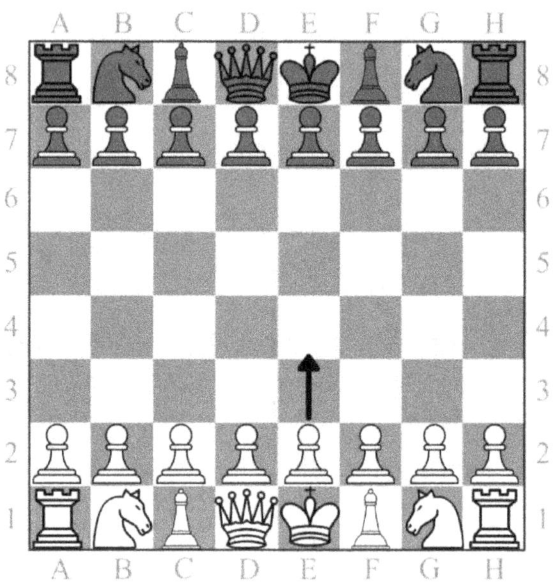

This move is very common in openings or first moves and is known as "King's Pawn Opening", its main objective is to control the center of the board and thus, allow the rapid development of our pieces.

We continue with "e5" the second term of the nomenclature: Now it is the turn of the player with the black pieces, who responds by also moving two spaces forward the pawn located on the e7 square; that is, he places it on the e5 square.

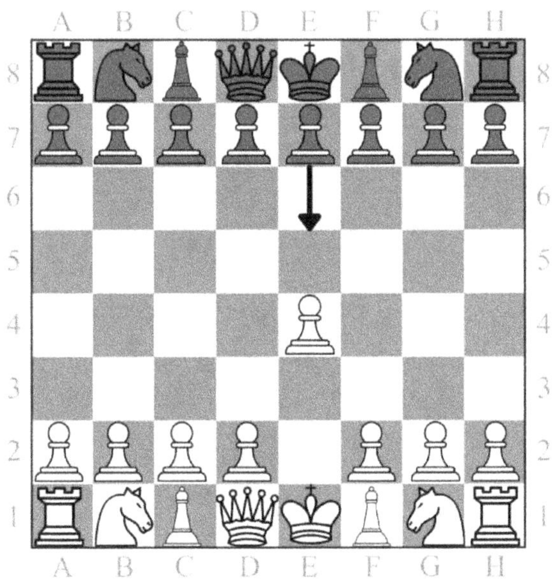

This move is called "King's Pawn Defense" and is a very common response to the King's Pawn opening. With this move, our opponent also seeks to take control of the center of the board and thus, establish a solid defense.

Following the sequence of terms, it is the turn of "2.Nf3": Again, it is the turn of the player of the white pieces; he moves the knight located on square g1 forward and to the left; that is, he places it on the square f3.

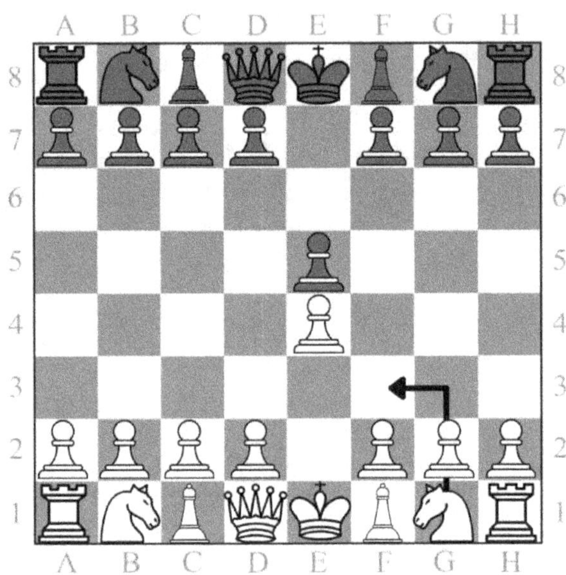

This move is known as the "Italian Defense" (which we will see in more detail in the next section) and attacks the black pawn on the e5 square. The main objective of this move is to develop a piece and control the center of the board.

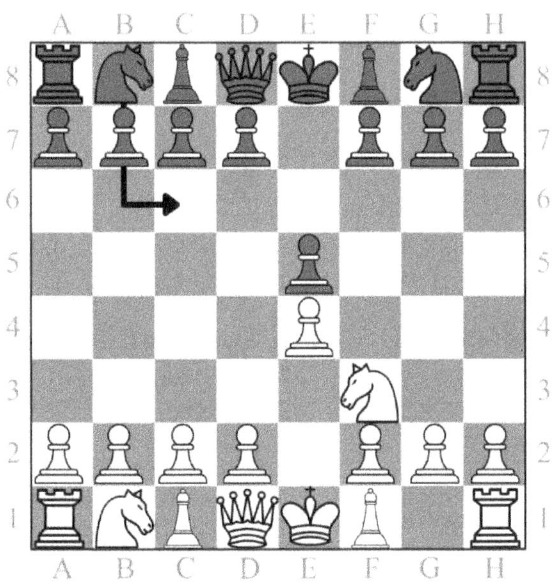

Then we have the term "Nc6": The player of the black pieces responds to the previous move of his opponent by moving forward and to the right his knight, located on square b8; that is, he places it on square c6.

With this move, the black pieces develop their knight, seek to control the center and defend their pawn on e5.

Finally, the term Bc4: The white player moves his bishop located on the c1 square to the c4 square; his objective with this is to develop that bishop and also to point towards the part of the board where the opponent's king is located and towards the f7 square, where that king could be in danger in the next moves.

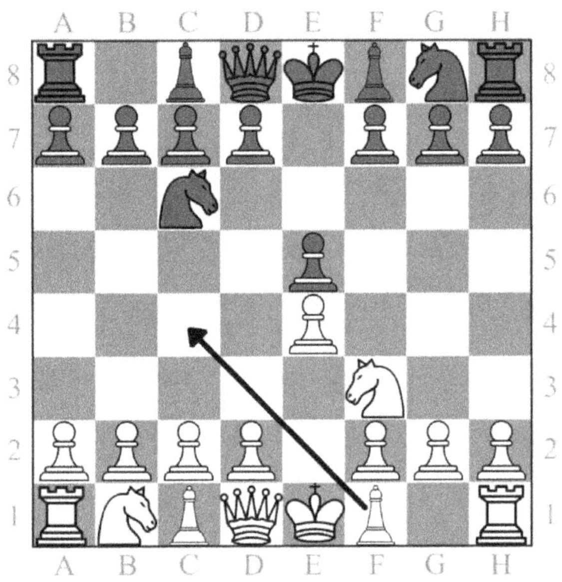

The Italian opening is a strategy that can be performed both by the player of the white pieces and the player of the black pieces.

In chess, there are many different openings, each one with its own strategies and characteristics; the Italian opening is only one of them. Playing it can lead to different alternatives and variants in the game, so it is important that you study and practice to improve your chess skills.

4.3. Sicilian defense

To begin with, let us remember that in the Italian opening, the player with the white pieces starts the game with moves to prepare for a good start.

In this opening, the white pieces start by moving the pawn on the e2 square to gain control of the center of the board from the beginning.

Now, let's imagine that the Sicilian Defense is like a wall that the player with the black pieces tries to build to protect himself and counterattack the player with the white pieces.

So, the Sicilian defense is the defensive approach to respond to the player's move with the white pieces, which is characterized by the initial moves: 1.e4 c5.

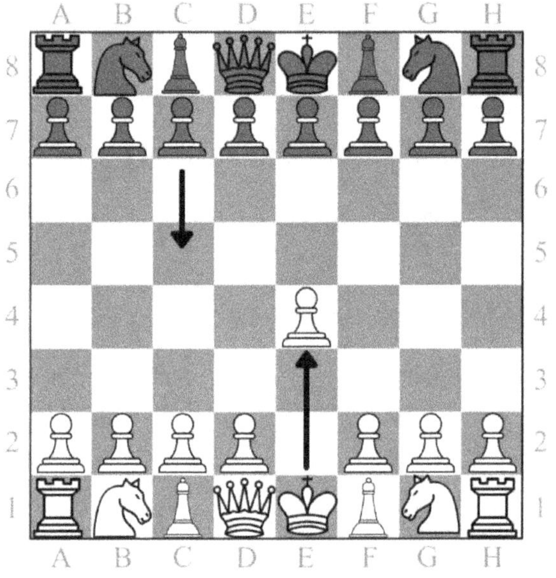

That is to say; if the white player started the game with 1.e4, the black player can respond to this advance by moving his own pawn to c5, thus controlling the d4 square and limiting his opponent's space in the center of the board.

The player with the white pieces can then continue with different moves, such as 2.Nf3 or 2.d4, and this can create several variants in the Sicilian defense.

Each variant has its own strategies and tactics; it is convenient that, as a chess player, you know and practice them to become familiar with them and thus, improve your game.

In this chapter, we learned how fundamental and important the openings are to establish a good base at the beginning of the game and prepare for the middle game. Knowing the openings and their basic principles will help you to make strategic decisions and create game plans.

Let's continue reading chapter 5, where we will learn new strategies and tactics for the development of the game, this time in the intermediate stage of the game.

We will learn about planning and strategy in the middlegame, the creation of attack plans and the relative value of pieces.

Chapter 5.

Half game

The middle game in chess is a crucial stage, as the pieces are developed and each of the players begin to form their strategic plans to achieve victory.

In this chapter, we will learn how to plan and execute moves during this phase of the game.

5.1. Planning and strategy in the midgame

In the game, to have an advantage over the other player, it is necessary to develop a solid strategy and establish intelligent plans.

During this mid-game, it is important to keep in mind several strategic aspects; these are some of those key points that will help you during this stage of the game:

Occupy the center of the board: Remember to occupy the squares in the heart of the board, d4, d5, e4 and e5, to have more space and better mobility.

Develop your pieces: Develop your pieces at the beginning; take your knights, bishops, rooks and queen out of their initial home and bring them into the game.

Protect your pieces: Prevent the opponent from capturing your pieces, always think of their safety and try not to make moves that endanger them.

Calculate your moves: Think about your moves before you make them, and anticipate your opponent's responses. Try to visualize several moves ahead in the game, so you can make the right decisions.

Control Open Lines: For your pieces, look for open columns or rows where there are no pawns, thus giving them more power and mobility.

Exchange Advantageous Pieces: If you have more pieces than your opponent, you could exchange some of them to be in a better position in the game. For example, if you have more knights and bishops than your opponent, you can look for opportunities to capture his pieces. By doing so, he will have fewer pieces on the board, giving you a numerical advantage, but if you are at a disadvantage, try to keep them on the board to create more opportunities.

Plan your attacks: Think about how you are going to attack your opponent's king, look for weaknesses in his positions, and try to create threats to checkmate him.

Evaluate the position: We will analyze the position of our pieces and those of the opponent to identify strengths and weaknesses. We will look for areas on the board where we can exert pressure and create opportunities to advance.

Create a plan: Once we evaluate the position, it is time to establish a strategic plan. This involves deciding which part of the board we want to control, how we will develop our pieces and which moves will bring us closer to our goal.

Improve our pieces: During the middle game, we will try to improve the position of our pieces. This means looking for opportunities to relocate them to more active squares, where they have greater reach and can exert more influence on the game.

Connecting the pieces: Another important objective is to connect our pieces. This implies coordinating them effectively to work as a team and support each other. A good coordination between our pieces will allow us to have a more harmonious and powerful game.

Chess is not only about moving pieces; it is also about thinking and having a clear strategy. By planning strategic moves and executing them in the middle game, you will make better decisions and increase your chances of winning.

Now that we have learned about planning and strategy in the midgame, you are ready to discover the next section. Continue reading and learn about creating plans of attack.

5.2. Creation of attack plans

The middle game is the perfect time to develop the attack on your opponent and put his king in trouble. Here are some things to remember when creating your attack plans:

Look at the position of your pieces on the board: Think which ones could make more powerful attacks if you move them to certain squares.

Identify which pieces protect the enemy king: This way, you will find an opportunity to attack it, either by removing or blocking the pieces that protect it.

Look for weaknesses in your opponent's defense: Look for weak squares around his king, where there are no other pieces to protect him; these squares can be a good target to attack.

Create threats: Move your pieces to threaten your opponent's pieces. If he feels he has one of his pieces in danger, he will look for a way to protect it or move it.

Coordinate your pieces: Try to make your pieces work as a team to make them stronger and more efficient.

Think about the next move: When planning an attack, anticipate how your opponent might respond. Anticipate his moves and think about how you are going to counter his next moves.

Be patient and flexible: Your attack plans may change because of your opponent's decisions. Be flexible and adjust your strategy if necessary.

Each game is different, and you will not always have to attack; you will also have to defend your pieces and protect your king.

In the next section of the book: "The relative value of the pieces" you will learn more about the power and importance of each piece in the game.

5.3. The relative value of the parts

In this section, we will discover how much the pieces are worth in chess and how this information helps us to make strategic decisions during the game.

In chess, each piece has an estimated numerical value that is used as a guide to evaluate the importance of each piece in the game; they are used to compare and understand the relative importance of the pieces during a game.

That is, this numerical rating is used by each player as a strategic reference to make decisions during the game.

The numerical value of the pieces is based on their ability to move, as well as their potential influence on the board.

Traditionally, it is assigned the value of:
- 1 point to the pawn.
- 3 points to the knight.
- 3 points to the bishop.
- 5 points to the tower.

- 9 points to the queen.

- The king, despite its vital importance, has no numerical value assigned to it, since its capture entails the immediate loss of the game.

With this information, a player can, for example, exchange a higher-value piece for a lower-value piece and gain a positional advantage by capturing a key opponent's piece.

However, it is important to note that the numerical value of the pieces is not absolute and may vary depending on the context of the game.

Other factors, such as pawn structure, board position and tactical opportunities, may also influence the evaluation of a position.

The numerical value of the pieces in chess evaluates the relative importance of each piece but does not calculate a final numerical score at the end of the game.

Continue reading with the last chapter of the book, where we will discover strategies and tactics for the final stages of the game, where there are fewer pieces.

Chapter 6.

Finals

The endgame stage is the last part of a chess game, where strategies and tactics become even more important.

This is the moment when the player needs to make the most of his resources and skills to achieve victory.

In this chapter, we will discover how to perform the final mate, which is the main objective of chess.

This last chapter is divided into two sections. In the first one, we will discover the most common endgames and the key techniques to win in this stage of the game. In the second section, we will learn the final move that assures the triumph: checkmate.

6.1. Basic endpoints

Endgames constitute the final stage of the chess game. By this time, there are few pieces left on the board; kings have a more active role in the game and strategy is important to obtain victory.

Some of the most common basic endings are:

King vs. King: This is the most basic ending; it is a "stalemate by stalemate" or "stalemate" draw where only the two kings remain on the board plus, in the event that both players continue the game without giving checkmate, the game can be prolonged for 50 consecutive moves until it is considered a draw by the 50 Moves Rule.

King and Pawn vs. King: In this ending, you have your king and one of your pawns against the other player's king. Try to advance your pawn to the last row and promote it to a more powerful piece. In this case, your king will be essential to protect your pawn from the attacks of the opposing king to ensure its coronation.

King and Rook vs. King: Here, you have your king and one of your rooks against the opponent's king. Use the rook to attack the opponent's king, so you can force him to unfavorable positions. In this case, the cooperation between your king and your rook is essential to achieve mate.

King and Queen vs. King: In this endgame, you have your king and queen against the enemy king. The queen is a powerful piece; she uses her power to corner the opposing king and seek mate.

King and Bishop vs. King: In this endgame, you have your king and one of your bishops against the opponent's king. Use your bishop's mobility to limit the enemy king's moves and look for mate.

There are other basic endings possible in chess, such as:

King and Pawn against King
King and Rook vs.
King and Queen against King
King and Bishop against King
King and Knight vs. King

King and two Knights against King

King and two Bishops against King

King and two Towers vs.

King and Rook vs. King and Bishop

King and Rook vs. King and Knight

King and Rook vs. King and two Knights

King and Rook against King and two Bishops

King and Queen against King and Bishop

King and Queen versus King and Knight

King and Queen vs. King and two Knights

King and Queen vs. King and two Bishops

These are some examples of the basic endgames possible in chess. Each presents unique strategic and tactical challenges; try to practice them and design a good strategy to win in each of them.

Remember that in the endgame, every move is crucial and patience and strategy are fundamental.

Now, it is time to continue with the Checkmate section. In this part, we will learn how to make the final move to ensure our victory in the game.

Read on and find out how to win a game of chess!

6.2. Checkmate

Checkmate occurs when a player's king is located in a position from which it can neither move nor escape capture on the next move. When this happens, the game ends and the player who succeeds in checkmate is the winner.

To understand this move, it is important to know how the king moves and how the other pieces are used to trap it. Here are some key moves you should know:

Movement of the king: The king can move one square at a time in any direction, forward, backward, sideways or diagonally. However, the king cannot move to a square that is threatened by an opponent's piece.

Checkmates: Several pieces can collaborate to checkmate the opposing king; the queen, the rook, the bishops and the knights are the most effective to achieve it.

Escape blocking: Try to block the possible escape squares of your opponent's king. This is achieved by interposing your own pieces or capturing the opponent's pieces that could both defend it.

Double attacks: A common checkmate tactic is to perform a double attack, where two of your pieces work together to threaten your opponent's king from different directions, leaving him with no escape options.

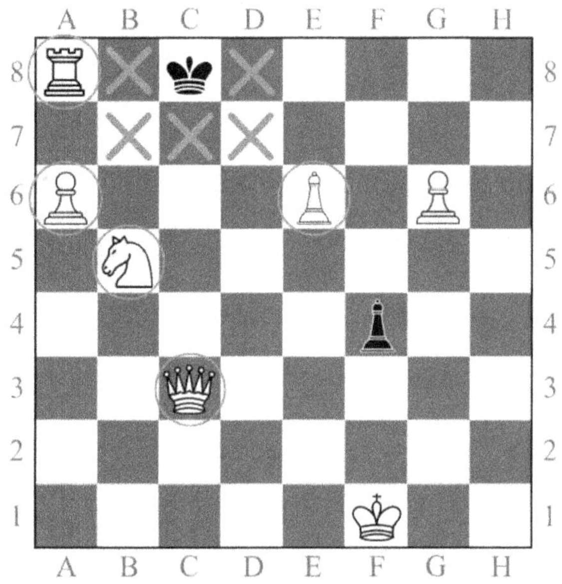

Remember that achieving a checkmate requires good planning and strategy, think carefully about each move and anticipate the possible responses of the opponent.

In this chapter, we discovered the final moments of the game of chess. We discovered the basic endgames and learned a little more about checkmate.

With this, I can only congratulate you for having reached the end of the book and having strengthened your strategic and tactical skills to face the challenge of the game until the last move.

Conclusion

Congratulations, little genius! You now have a valuable treasure trove of chess knowledge.

With this book, we have discovered the basic rules of chess, how to move each piece on the board and the strategies to win.

We learned about openings, tactics and endgames, as well as the importance of planning and making strategic decisions.

Chess is more than just a game; it is a powerful tool to develop skills such as logical thinking, concentration, decision making and creativity. By playing it, you exercise your mind and become a strategist.

Keep practicing and playing with friends, family or in tournaments. As you continue to learn and play, you will become a true master.

Remember that the adventure of chess never ends. There will always be more to learn and more games to play.

Recommendations for parents and teachers

To the parents and teachers of little chess geniuses, I would like to give the following recommendations:

Motivate continued interest: Encourage your child or student to discover chess, even if he or she has already read this book. Support him or her to keep playing and practicing.

Play together: Play chess with your child or student; this will allow him/her to practice what he/she has learned and will strengthen his/her strategic skills.

Establish challenges: Propose chess challenges to your child or student, such as solving tactical problems, looking for combinations or even playing timed games; this way, you will motivate his progress, which will help him to consolidate what he has learned and improve his skills.

Encourage fair play and respect: Teach your child or student about the importance of playing fair, respecting the rules and showing respect for the opponent. Chess is a valuable opportunity to develop values.

Support participation in tournaments and competitions: Encourage your child or student to participate in local tournaments or school chess competitions; this will give them real game experience, they will be able to meet other players and will motivate them to continue improving.

Celebrate achievements: Recognize and celebrate your child's or student's chess accomplishments. It may be a tournament victory, a successful solution to a tactical problem, or their dedication and effort to improve. This will motivate them and build their confidence.

Encourage fellowship: Encourage your child or student to share his knowledge of chess with other children; he can teach them basic moves, solve problems together or even organize friendly games. This will encourage both collaboration and companionship.

Chess, besides being a game, is a powerful educational tool. With your support and motivation, you will help your child or student to develop cognitive, strategic and emotional skills useful in every aspect of his or her life.

Keep supporting the little chess geniuses on their journey to greatness!

Free course and chess platform for children

https://www.chesskid.com/home

Your help means a lot

If you liked this book, one of the best things you could do for me would be to leave a review on the website where you bought it. It won't take you long, but it would be great if you could spare those minutes for me.

If you give my work a high rating, more people will see it and, in turn, it will improve their lives, health and happiness.

May your trip be full of fun and growth,
Pavel Ganchev